Nita Mehta's
Sandwiches

Nita Mehta

B.Sc. (Home Science), M.Sc. (Food and Nutrition), Gold Medalist

Nita Mehta's
Sandwiches

© Copyright 2007 **SNAB** Publishers Pvt Ltd

WORLD RIGHTS RESERVED: The contents - all recipes, photographs and drawings are original and copyrighted. No portion of this book shall be reproduced, stored in a retrieval system or transmitted by any means, electronic, mechanical, photocopying, recording or otherwise, without the written permission of the publishers.

While every precaution is taken in the preparation of this book, the publishers and the author assume no responsibility for errors or omissions. Neither is any liability assumed for damages resulting from the use of information contained herein.

TRADEMARKS ACKNOWLEDGED: Trademarks used, if any, are acknowledged as trademarks of their respective owners. These are used as reference only and no trademark infringement is intended upon. Ajinomoto (monosodium glutamate, MSG) is a trademark of Aji-no-moto company of Japan. Use it sparingly if you must as a flavour enhancer.

ISBN 978-81-7869-182-4

Exclusive Distributor:

AM PRODUCTIONS
DIVISION OF: INFORMATION SCIENCE INDUSTRIES (CANADA) LIMITED

1169 Parisien St., Ottawa, Ont., K1B 4W4,
Tel: 613.745.3098 Fax: 613.745.7533
e-mail: amproductions@rogers.com
web: www.amproductions.ca

Published by:

SNAB
Publishers Pvt. Ltd.
3A/3 Asaf Ali Road,
New Delhi - 110002
Tel: 23252948, 23250091
Telefax: 91-11-23250091
INDIA

Editorial and Marketing office:
E-159, Greater Kailash-II, N.Delhi-48
Fax: 91-11-29225218, 29229558
Tel: 91-11-29214011, 29218727, 29218574
E-Mail: nitamehta@email.com, nitamehta@nitamehta.com
Website: http://www.nitamehta.com
Website: http://www.snabindia.com

Printed at:

PRESSTECH LITHO PVT. LTD., NEW DELHI

Price: $ 5.95

Contents

Introduction 4
International Conversion Guide 5

Pan Crisp & Toasted 6

Chicken Burgers 7
Italian Pesto Sandwiches 8
Crusty Chicken Salad Rolls 10
Minty Hawaiian Hotdogs 12
Bacon and Asparagus Rolls 14
Club Sandwiches 16

Low Cal Sandwiches 18

Baby Corn & Mint Slices 19
Tropical Tuna Salad Rolls 20
Yogurt Drops 23
Lebanese Sandwiches 25
Creamy Shrimp Sandwiches 26
Grilled Ricotta Focaccia 28

Open Sandwiches 30

Cajun Shrimp on Toast 31
Broccoli & Corn Footlong 32
Sausage on Buns 34
Pizza Pockets 36
Cheesy Spinach Toasties 37

Sandwiches for Children 38

Salami Sandwiches 39
Asian Chicken Croissants 40
Ham Sandwich Loaf 42
Sandwich Faces 44
Cheese Pockets 46
Bean Teen Burgers 47

Glossary 48

Introduction

Sandwiches are no longer tea-time treats. With different kinds of breads available and more so, because of whole wheat and other healthy options of bread, sandwiches make a complete, well balanced meal. We have used vegetables, meat, processed cheese or paneer, beans, natural herbs to make the sandwiches healthy and delicious at the same time. The fresh, light and innovative recipes are surely going to be appreciated by all your family members. These days, the range of sandwiches is really huge. You'll have a choice for each member of your family, be it a child, an adult or an older person.

You can choose from pan grilled to toasted sandwiches; from sandwiches for children to low cal sandwiches. Open sandwiches can be served as interesting starters at a party too. All recipes are delicious and quick to prepare. Every recipe is tried and tested and guaranteed to satisfy you.

Nita Mehta

INTERNATIONAL CONVERSION GUIDE

These are not exact equivalents; they've been rounded-off to make measuring easier.

WEIGHTS & MEASURES

METRIC	IMPERIAL
15 g	½ oz
30 g	1 oz
60 g	2 oz
90 g	3 oz
125 g	4 oz (¼ lb)
155 g	5 oz
185 g	6 oz
220 g	7 oz
250 g	8 oz (½ lb)
280 g	9 oz
315 g	10 oz
345 g	11 oz
375 g	12 oz (¾ lb)
410 g	13 oz
440 g	14 oz
470 g	15 oz
500 g	16 oz (1 lb)
750 g	24 oz (1½ lb)
1 kg	30 oz (2 lb)

LIQUID MEASURES

METRIC	IMPERIAL
30 ml	1 fluid oz
60 ml	2 fluid oz
100 ml	3 fluid oz
125 ml	4 fluid oz
150 ml	5 fluid oz (¼ pint/1 gill)
190 ml	6 fluid oz
250 ml	8 fluid oz
300 ml	10 fluid oz (½ pint)
500 ml	16 fluid oz
600 ml	20 fluid oz (1 pint)
1000 ml	1¾ pints

CUPS & SPOON MEASURES

METRIC	IMPERIAL
1 ml	¼ tsp
2 ml	½ tsp
5 ml	1 tsp
15 ml	1 tbsp
60 ml	¼ cup
125 ml	½ cup
250 ml	1 cup

HELPFUL MEASURES

METRIC	IMPERIAL
3 mm	1/8 in
6 mm	¼ in
1 cm	½ in
2 cm	¾ in
2.5 cm	1 in
5 cm	2 in
6 cm	2½ in
8 cm	3 in
10 cm	4 in
13 cm	5 in
15 cm	6 in
18 cm	7 in
20 cm	8 in
23 cm	9 in
25 cm	10 in
28 cm	11 in
30 cm	12 in (1ft)

HOW TO MEASURE

When using the graduated metric measuring cups, it is important to shake the dry ingredients loosely into the required cup. Do not tap the cup on the table, or pack the ingredients into the cup unless otherwise directed. Level top of cup with a knife. When using graduated metric measuring spoons, level top of spoon with a knife. When measuring liquids in the jug, place jug on a flat surface, check for accuracy at eye level.

OVEN TEMPERATURE

These oven temperatures are only a guide. Always check the manufacturer's manual.

	°C (Celsius)	°F (Fahrenheit)	Gas Mark
Very low	120	250	1
Low	150	300	2
Moderately low	160	325	3
Moderate	180	350	4
Moderately high	190	375	5
High	200	400	6
Very high	230	450	7

Pan Crisp
& Toasted

Chicken Burgers

Fresh breadcrumbs add body to these fantastic burgers – pan-fry and serve with all the trimmings between buttery crisp buns.

Makes 4

INGREDIENTS

315 g/10 oz ground chicken
4 soft burger buns, 1 tbsp butter
½ cup finely chopped onion
½ tsp minced or crushed garlic
1 slice bread
1 tsp Worcestershire sauce, optional
1 tbsp cornstarch, 1 egg
1 tsp salt and ¼ tsp pepper, or to taste
4 lettuce leaves, 4 tomato slices*
1 tbsp mustard, some mayonnaise to dot

METHOD

1. Tear 1 slice of bread into pieces. Grind in a mixer to get ½ cup fresh bread crumbs. Keep aside.

2. Melt 1 tbsp butter in a frying pan. Add chopped onion and garlic. Cook until onions turn soft, for about 3-4 minutes.

3. Remove from heat. Mix ground chicken, bread crumbs, egg and cornstarch. Add salt and pepper and mix well. Mix in worcesterchire sauce if you like.

4. On a floured board, form the mixture into 4 round burgers.

5. Heat some oil in a frying pan and fry the burger on low medium heat for about 3-4 minutes, about 2 minutes on each side. See that they get cooked from inside.

6. Split the buns, toss in some butter in a pan till soft. Remove from pan & spread some mustard paste on the bottom piece.

7. Place a lettuce leaf, then the burger and a slice of tomato on each. Top with some mayonnaise. Cover with the other piece of bun. Serve.

Italian Pesto Sandwiches

Pesto sauce with basil and pine nuts; a marinade of balsamic vinegar and oregano – grasp the Italian country side between two slices of bread!

Makes 6

INGREDIENTS

100 g/3 oz mozzarella cheese, preferably fresh mozzarella - cut into thin slices
1 small cucumber
2 tbsp balsamic vinegar
½ tsp oregano, ¼ tsp of salt
2 tomatoes - sliced thinly
1 tbsp sliced olives, 6 slices of bread
some salt to sprinkle
3 tbsp pesto, ready made or home made, recipe given below

METHOD

1. Take out a long peel from the cucumber with a vegetable peeler. Roll the strip of peel and pass through a tooth pick. Keep aside for the garnish. Now cut the cucumber into thin slices. Cut the cheese block also into thin slices.

2. In a bowl mix balsamic vinegar, oregano & salt. Add the mozzarella slices and 10-12 slices of cucumber. Mix well turning sides so that everything gets coated with the balsamic vinegar marinade.

3. Spread ½ tbsp pesto on each slice of bread. Put 2 slices of marinated cheese on a slice. Arrange a few olive slices. Place 4 slices of tomatoes. Sprinkle salt and pepper. Put a few cucumber slices on the tomatoes. Press the second slice on it, keeping the pesto side inside. Trim sides.

4. Serve as it is or grill till crisp. Cut into 2 pieces to serve. Pierce the cucumber-peel toothpick through an olive or a piece of tomato and press on the sandwich.

PESTO SAUCE

1½ cups basil leaves or fresh coriander
2 tbsp pinenuts (*chilgoze*) or walnuts
2 flakes garlic - chopped
¼ cup grated parmesan or cheddar cheese, 4 tbsp olive oil
½ tsp salt, ¼ tsp freshly crushed pepper

Put basil, nuts, garlic, cheese, salt and pepper in a mixer and grind to a paste. With the motor still running, add the oil in a steady stream until well combined. Store the pesto in the fridge in a bottle. Pour some olive oil in the bottle, over the top, to prevent the basil from turning brown.

Crusty Chicken Salad Rolls

Diced cooked chicken mixed with apples and green onions and tossed in a milky almond dressing – fill this into crusty bread rolls and enjoy!

Makes 2

INGREDIENTS

2 crusty bread rolls
125 g/4 oz chicken, 1 tsp oil
½ apple - peeled, cored and chopped
1 egg - hard-boiled and chopped
1 spring onion - diagonally sliced along with the greens

DRESSING

15 almonds - roasted and crushed
5 tbsp olive oil
3 tbsp chopped parsley or coriander
3 tbsp milk
2 tbsp water
¾ tsp pepper
¾ tsp salt

METHOD

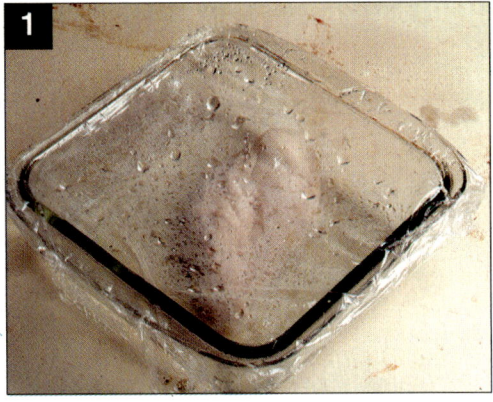

1. Place the chicken with ¼ cup water, 1 tsp oil and ¼ tsp salt in a dish. Mix well. Cover with a plastic wrap and microwave for 2½ minutes. Leave chicken in the microwave for 5 minutes to get fully cooked on standing. Drain chicken. Discard bones. Cut chicken into pieces. Keep chicken pieces aside.

2. To make the dressing, place all ingredients of the dressing in a mixer. Process to combine to a rough mixture.

3. Mix chicken, apple, egg, spring onion and the prepared dressing. Mix well. Season salad according to your taste

4. Cut rolls in half. Pile the bottom with salad, then place other half on top. Warm in a microwave for 30 seconds. Serve.

Minty Hawaiian Hotdogs

Thick yogurt sweetened with honey and mint coats the fruits and veggies that are filled into this new-age, healthy hotdog!

Makes 4

INGREDIENTS

4 hot dog buns
¾ cup yogurt - hang for 15 minutes in a muslin cloth
1 tbsp mint paste or mint chutney
1 slice of pineapple, fresh or tinned - chopped
½ cup peas, ¾ cup corn
1 firm tomato - cut into 4 pieces, remove pulp and cut into thin strips
4 tbsp grated cheddar cheese
salt, pepper to taste, 1 tsp honey, optional

METHOD

1. Hang yogurt in a muslin cloth for 15 minutes. Beat well till smooth.

2. To the hung yogurt, add the mint paste or chutney. Add pineapple bits, corn and peas. Mix well. Add salt, pepper to taste. If the yogurt tastes sour, add a tsp of honey.

3. Cut each bun into two halves lengthways.

4. Spread the pineapple-pea-corn mixture on the bottom piece of the bun and top it with tomato strips. Sprinkle 1 tbsp cheese on the tomatoes. Cover with the second piece of bun. If you like, spread some butter on the top half of the bun before placing on the lower portion.

5. Heat the buns on a non stick pan in 1 tbsp butter till crisp or put under a grill for 5 minutes or till crisp.

MINT CHUTNEY

½ cup chopped poodina (*mint leaves*)
1 cup chopped coriander (*hara dhania*)
1 onion - chopped
2 green chillies - chopped
1½ tsp lemon juice
1½ tsp sugar, ½ tsp salt
1 tbsp olive oil

Wash coriander and mint leaves. Grind all ingredients with just enough water to get the right consistency of the chutney. Store in the fridge for a week or 10 days.

Bacon and Asparagus Rolls

An asparagus stalk is rolled in three blankets: a cheese slice, a thin bread slice, and bacon. The roll is gently pan-fried till melting and crisp.

Makes 4

INGREDIENTS

4 bacon rashers
4 slices of bread
4 cheese slices
8 stalks of asparagus or tender green beans
butter and mustard - enough to spread
1 tbsp flour (*maida*) - to dust rolling pin
salt and pepper to sprinkle

4 & 5

METHOD

1. Cut about 1" of the lower tough end of the asparagus. If using beans, string the beans. Boil 4 cups water with 1 tsp salt and 1 tsp sugar. Add the asparagus or beans. Boil for 1 minute. Remove from water and keep blanched vegetables aside.

2. Dust the rolling pin with some flour. Cut the edges of the bread. Roll bread slices with a rolling pin (*belan*) to make the slices thinner.

3. Spread the slices with butter on one side and mustard on the other side.

4. Place 1 cheese slice on the mustard side, top with 2 asparagus or beans, showing a little outside the bread. Sprinkle salt and pepper. Roll up tightly.

5. Wrap bacon all around the bread. Secure with toothpicks, most of the length being inserted in the roll.

6. Pan fry the roll on a greased non stick pan for 2-3 minutes, turning sides. Alternately, grill in a hot oven for 4 minutes, or until bacon is cooked. Turn side once in between.

Club Sandwiches

Toasted bread sandwiched with sauted slices of potatoes, cucumber & cabbage leaves.

Makes 4

INGREDIENTS

6 bread slices, 2 tbsp butter
2 potatoes
1 small cucumber - sliced thinly
2 cabbage leaves - tear each into 4 pieces
1-2 firm tomatoes - cut into slices
salt and pepper to taste
4 cheese slices
some mayonnaise - enough to spread

METHOD

1. Wash potatoes and place wet potatoes in the microwave. Microwave for 5 minutes. Remove from microwave and peel after they cool down. If you like, boil the potatoes till just done. Cut potatoes into ¼" thick round slices.

2. Heat 2 tbsp butter in a big nonstick pan. Put a few slices of potatoes on it. Turn when the under side is light brown and then shift to the sides. Put more slices in the centre and brown them. Repeat with all other potato slices. Let potatoes be on the sides of the pan.

3. Place the cabbage leaves also on the hot pan. Saute till black patches appear on the leaves. Remove from heat. Leave everything in the pan.

4. Lightly toast the bread slices. Spread mayonnaise on one side of the slices.

5. On a toast place some cabbage leaves on the mayonnaise.

6. Cover the leaves with potato slices. Sprinkle salt and pepper. Put tomato slices over the potatoes.

7. Spread some butter on a toast, such that it has butter on one side and mayonnaise on the other side. Place toast over the tomatoes. Arrange 3-4 cucumber slices on it. Sprinkle some salt and pepper. Top with a cheese slice. Cover with another toasted slice, keeping the mayonnaise side down. Press gently. Cut into two pieces. Serve.

Baby Corn & Mint Slices

French bread is topped with loads of fusion flavour – soya sauce and vinegar; paneer and mint, garlic and oregano.

Makes 15-18

INGREDIENTS

1 French Loaf or garlic bread - cut into ¼" thick diagonal slices
½ cup feta or *paneer* - grated
2 tbsp chopped mint

BABY CORN TOPPING
150g/5 oz baby corns - sliced into rounds (1½ cups)
2 tsp vinegar, 2 tsp soya sauce
1 tsp red chilli sauce
2 tbsp cornstarch dissolved in ½ cup water
½ tsp salt, ½ tsp pepper

TOMATO SPREAD
6-8 flakes garlic - crushed
1 tsp oregano
½ cup ready made tomato puree
2 tbsp tomato ketchup
½ tsp salt and ½ tsp pepper, or to taste

METHOD

1. To prepare the tomato spread, mix all the ingredients and cook on low heat for about 5 minutes, till thick. Keep aside.

2. To prepare the topping, mix all ingredients, except the baby corns in a heavy bottomed pan or *kadhai* and then add the sliced baby corns. Keep on low heat for 3-4 minutes and cook stirring continuously till the sauce coats the baby corns and they get cooked a little.

3. Spread some tomato spread on the slices. Arrange some baby corns in sauce. Press.

4. Grate some *paneer* finely over it. Sprinkle some mint, crushed peppercorns and some salt on the paneer.

5. To serve, grill at 200°C for 7-8 minutes till a little crisp. Do not over grill otherwise they turn too hard.

Note: *If baby corns are not available, 1 cup of frozen or tinned corn kernels may be substituted.*

Tropical Tuna Salad Rolls

Here's a radical transformation for the humble tuna sandwich – it is glamorised with mango strips and dressed with honey-green chilli dressing.

Makes 4

INGREDIENTS

4 hot dog rolls
1 small tin tuna, 185 g/6 oz
1 ripe mango or 2 slices of pineapple - cut into thick strips
1 spring onion - chopped with the greens
1 tbsp finely chopped parsley or coriander
8 tsp mustard, preferably whole grain

DRESSING
1 tbsp chopped green chillies
2 tbsp lemon juice or vinegar
4 tbsp honey, 8 tbsp milk
1 tsp salt, 1 tsp paprika

METHOD

1. Drain the tuna and mix in a bowl with spring onion and parsley.

2. Mix all ingredients of the dressing in a small spice grinder. Pour the dressing on the tuna mixture.

3. Cut the rolls into 2 halves horizontally. Spread a tsp of mustard paste on each piece of bread.

4. Top mustard with some tuna mixture. Arrange the mango slices on top.

5. Cover with the the other piece of bread. Press lightly. Grill for 4-5 minutes in a hot oven till crisp.

Yogurt Drops

Finely chopped salad veggies are tossed in yogurt then filled into unusual round sandwiches. Serve as small bites in between meals for a low calorie diet.

Serves 3-4

INGREDIENTS

12 slices bread - toasted and cut into rounds with a big cookie cutter
1 cup yogurt - hang for 1-2 hours in a muslin cloth
1 tsp mustard, 1 tsp tomato ketchup
¼ cup grated cabbage
¼ cup grated carrot
¼ cup finely chopped cucumber
½ tsp salt, ½ tsp pepper or to taste
¼ tsp sugar, optional

METHOD

1. Cut toasted bread slices into 12 rounds. Again, cut 6 rounds like a doughnut, using the lid of a small bottle or a tiny cookie cutter. Keep aside.

2. Beat hung yogurt in a bowl till smooth. Add tomato ketchup and mustard.

3. Add cabbage, carrot, cucumber, salt and pepper. Mix well. Add a little sugar, if needed.

4. Spread the yogurt on a full round of bread. Top with a doughnut-shaped round of bread. Put a spoon of yogurt mixture in the hole. Dot with mustard or ketchup.

Lebanese Sandwiches

Salad veggies are marinated in lemon juice and olive oil then grilled and tucked into pocket bread – marvellous tastes and textures to lighten your mood.

Makes 8

INGREDIENTS

2 pita breads or pizza bases
1 red bell pepper
1 green bell pepper
8 big mushrooms
1 tbsp lemon juice, 2 tbsp olive oil
½ tsp crushed or minced garlic
½ tsp cinnamon, ½ tsp salt
½ tsp freshly crushed pepper

SPREAD
3 tbsp cream cheese/cheese spread
2 tbsp yogurt
a pinch of salt and pepper, or to taste

METHOD

1. Cut the bell peppers into 1" squares. Slice the mushrooms thickly.

2. Mix together lemon juice, olive oil, garlic, cinnamon, salt and pepper. Pour over the vegetables in the bowl. Mix well and keep aside to marinate for 10 minutes. Put vegetables on a baking tray and grill for about 10 minutes or till the skin of the vegetables turn blackish. If you like, you can grill the vegetables in a pan, without stirring too much.

3. Mix together cheese and yogurt in a small bowl. Add salt and pepper to taste. Keep aside.

4. Cut each bread into 2 halves. Open up the bread from the cut edge, like a pocket. Spread ¼ of the cheese and yogurt spread, inside on each bottom piece of the bread.

5. Spread ¼ of the vegetables on the yogurt spread. Press lightly.

6. Keep on a hot pan or *tawa* and cook for about 1-2 minutes on each side. Serve as it is or cut into half to get 2 triangular pieces. Serve.

Creamy Shrimp Sandwiches

A well-flavoured yogurt spread combines with shrimps sautéed in butter and rosemary – what a unique filling for these scrumptious sandwiches!

Serves 2-3

INGREDIENTS

4 medium - sized shrimps - cleaned and deveined, 1 tbsp butter
4 slices of firm brown bread - toasted in a toaster
¾ cup yoghurt - tie in a muslin cloth for 15 minutes
1 tsp oregano, 2 tsp tomato ketchup
¾ tsp salt, 1 tsp pepper to taste
4 tbsp chopped onion
4 tbsp chopped bell peppers
1 tsp dried rosemary
few lettuce leaves

METHOD

1. Beat hung yoghurt till smooth. Mix bell pepper and onion into the yoghurt. Add oregano, tomato ketchup, salt and pepper.

2. Saute shrimps in 1 tbsp butter with dried rosemary and a little salt and pepper for about 2 minutes or till they turn whitish and tails turn orangish. Do not over cook shrimps.

3. Arrange lettuce leaves on a slice of bread. Place yoghurt mixture on the lettuce. Spread it a little. Place a shrimp on it. Serve.

Grilled Ricotta Focaccia

Wholegrain mustard and ricotta/paneer balance each other in this enchanting garden of a sandwich, with its rows of beautiful vegetables.

Serves 2

INGREDIENTS

5" square or round focaccia bread
3 tbsp wholegrain mustard
2 - 3 tomatoes - sliced
1 small green bell pepper - cut into strips
8 mushrooms - sliced

MIX TOGETHER

½ cup roughly crumbled ricotta cheese or *paneer*
2 tsp any fresh herb (rosemary/thyme/basil/corinader)
½ tsp freshly ground black pepper
½ tsp salt, or to taste

METHOD

1. Boil 2 cups water with 1 tsp lemon juice and 1 tsp salt. Add mushrooms and boil for 2 minutes. Remove from water. Pat dry on a kitchen towel. Cut into slices. Keep aside.

2. Split focaccia bread horizontally and toast lightly under a preheated grill or on a pan. Spread mustard on both the pieces of bread.

3. Place tomatoes, green bell pepper slices and mushrooms on the lower piece. Sprinkle salt and pepper.

4. Mix ricotta cheese, black pepper and salt. Add any fresh herb.

5. Sprinkle ricotta mixture on the vegetables. Cover with the other piece of bread.

6. Warm under a preheated grill for 3 minutes or until heated through and slightly brown.

Open Sandwiches

Cajun Shrimp on Toast

Spread tuna and mayonnaise on toast, cover with pan-fried shrimps, and sprinkle with paprika and cloves – a world-class creation!

Makes 5

INGREDIENTS

5 bread slices - toasted
¾ cup small shrimps, ¼ tsp minced garlic
1 tsp paprika powder
2 cloves (*laung*) - crushed
1 can (185 g/6 oz) tuna - flaked (1 cup)
¼ cup finely chopped celery or coriander
1 tsp lemon juice
4 tbsp mayonnaise
1 tbsp oil
a few bell pepper strips

METHOD

1. Combine flaked tuna, celery, lemon juice and mayonnaise.
2. Pan-fry shrimps with minced garlic in 1 tbsp oil for 2-3 minutes or till done. Sprinkle clove powder and paprika powder.
3. Spread tuna in mayonnaise on each toast.
4. Place shrimps and bell pepper strips. Sprinkle paprika powder again. Serve as it is or cut a toast into half to serve.

Broccoli & Corn Footlong

Colourful veggies are trapped in melted cheese – a taste-pleasure enhanced by chilli flakes and fennel seeds.

Serves 4

INGREDIENTS

1 french loaf - cut into half horizontally
2 tsp mustard paste

FLAVOURED BUTTER
4 tbsp softened butter
½ tsp black pepper
2-3 flakes garlic - chopped and crushed
½ tsp fennel seeds (*saunf*) - crushed

TOPPING
1 tbsp butter
4 tbsp cream cheese/cheese spread
1½ cups corn
1 cup tiny florets of broccoli
1 cup finely chopped onion
1 tsp salt
1 tsp pepper to taste
¾ cup grated mozzarella cheese
1 tsp oregano
1 tsp red chilli flakes
8-10 cherry tomatoes - split into halves

METHOD

1. Mix all ingredients given under flavoured butter till smooth.

2. Cut the french loaf horizontally to get 2 long pieces.

3. Butter both pieces with flavoured butter. Spread some mustard paste on the buttered footlong and keep aside.

4. To prepare the topping heat 1 tbsp butter in a pan. Add onion and broccoli. Saute till vegetables turn soft. Add corn, salt & pepper. Stir well to mix. Remove from heat. Add cheese spread/cream cheese to the hot mixture.

5. Spread broccoli-corn filling on the buttered foot long.

6. Sprinkle grated mozzarella over it and sprinkle some oregano and red chilli flakes. Top with cherry tomatoes.

7. At serving time, bake at 180°C/350°F for 10-12 minutes or till cheese melts and the bread turns crisp.

8. To serve, cut into 1½" thick slices.

Sausage on Buns

Hungry stomachs are going to relish this hearty mixture of baked beans and sausages presented in a bun-bowl – grilled till the cheese topping melts deliciously.

Serves 4-5

INGREDIENTS

6 breakfast sausages (chicken or pork)
4 round burger buns, some butter to brush
1¼ cups baked beans (200 g/7 oz)
1½ tsp tabasco sauce
2 tsp worcestershire sauce
¾ tsp salt, ½ tsp pepper
½ yellow or green bell pepper - chopped finely (½ cup)
2 tbsp chopped parsley or coriander
½ cup grated cheddar cheese

METHOD

1. Split 4 sausages into 2 pieces lengthways to get 8 pieces. Place the cut pieces of sausages in a nonstick pan and cook for a minute over very low heat until brown.

2. Chop the remaining 2 sausages.

3. To the beans, add the chopped sausages, the sauces, salt & pepper. Add bell pepper & parsley or coriander.

4. Cut each bun into half. Scoop out each piece of bun leaving a border of ½" all around. Brush the top and sides of bread with some butter.

5. Fill the buns with the bean mixture.

6. Arrange sausage halves on top. Top with grated cheese.

7. Grill in preheated oven for 4-5 minutes or till cheese melts. Serve hot.

Note : *Can use ham or bacon instead of sausages. Trim the fat of bacon, cut into pieces and saute in a pan.*

Pizza Pockets

Inside these pockets you will find veggies and sausages. On the outer surface you will find a layer of grilled cheese.

Serves 8

INGREDIENTS

2 thick pizza bases
4 sausages - thinly sliced diagonally
1 bell pepper - cut into thin strips
3-4 spring onions - sliced thinly
1 cup corn
2-3 tbsp tomato puree
salt & pepper to taste
2 tbsp butter
some lettuce leaves

TOPPING
1 tbsp butter
1 cup grated mozzarella cheese
1 tsp red chilli flakes
1 tsp dried oregano

METHOD

1. Cut pizza base into half. Slit open the cut side with the tip of a knife to make a deep pocket without damaging. Butter the top of the pizzas and grill till slightly crisp.

2. Push a small lettuce leaf into the pocket if you wish. Keep aside.

3. Heat butter in a non stick pan. Add spring onions and bell peppers. Saute for ½ minute. Add the sausages. Stir for a minute. Add the corn, tomato puree, pinch of salt & pepper and cook till puree dries and coats the mixture. Remove from heat.

4. Fill the pizza pockets with the mixture. Slightly butter the top of the pizza again and sprinkle grated cheese, chilli flakes and oregano.

5. Heat oven. Place the stuffed pizza on a greased tray. Grill for 3-4 minutes till the cheese on top melts.

6. Cut each half into 2 pieces to get 4 pieces from each pizza. Serve hot.

Cheesy Spinach Toasties

Spinach and cheese compliment each other perfectly – you will drool over these tempting toasties!

Serves 4-5

INGREDIENTS

4 slices bread
1½ tbsp butter
2-3 flakes garlic - crushed (½ tsp)
100 g/3 oz leaves of spinach - washed & shredded (¾ cup)
1½ cups ricotta or grated *paneer*
5 tbsp grated mozzarella or pizza cheese
1 tbsp chopped coriander/cilantro
¼ tsp salt and pepper or taste
½ tsp red chilli flakes

METHOD

1. Wash and shred spinach leaves into thin ribbons.

2. Heat butter in a pan. Add garlic and stir. Add spinach and cook till all the moisture of the spinach evaporates. Remove from heat.

3. Add ricotta or grated *paneer*, coriander/cilantro and 4 tbsp grated mozzarella cheese to the cooked spinach and mix well. Add salt and pepper.

4. Toast the slices and spread the mixture on the toasts. Sprinkle some mozzarella cheese. Sprinkle some red chilli flakes too.

5. Put under a grill for 2-3 minutes for the cheese to melt. Cut each slice into 2-4 triangles.

Sandwiches
For Children

Salami Sandwiches

Traditional combinations win every time – the popularity of this sandwich proves it.
Serves 2

INGREDIENTS

2 slices whole wheat bread - toasted in a toaster and buttered
2 lettuce or cabbage leaves
4 slices of salami
2 tbsp shredded cabbage mixed with 2 tbsp of mayonnaise
a few onion rings - separated
2- 3 cherry tomatoes- split into two
or
1 tomato cut into wedges - deseeded
paprika powder, optional

METHOD

1. Spread butter on the toasted slices.

2. Cover with a lettuce leaf.

3. Arrange 2 salami slices on each piece. Arrange some cabbage-mayonnaise mix on the salami.

4. Garnish with onion rings and cherry tomato or wedges of tomato. Sprinkle paprika.

Asian Chicken Croissants

A great partnership between shredded chicken and mango chutney layered inside a golden croissant – the right formula for success.

Serves 4

INGREDIENTS

250g/8 oz chicken
4 croissants
2 tbsp coarsely crushed almonds or peanuts
4 tbsp mango chutney
1 cup finely chopped cucumber
½ cup sliced onion
1 tsp ground cumin (*jeera*)
½ tsp salt, ½ tsp pepper to taste

METHOD

1. Place chicken in a microproof dish. Add ¼ cup water and ¼ tsp salt. Cover with a plastic wrap and microwave for 4 minutes. Remove from microwave and let it cool. Shred chicken into small pieces.

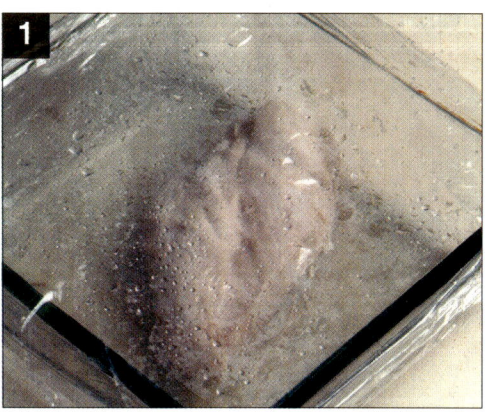

2. Mix chutney, chicken, nuts, cucumber, onion, ground cumin, salt and pepper in a bowl.

3. Slit croissant horizontally leaving the end intact.

4. Put the chicken filling in the slit croissant. Microwave for 10 seconds to serve.

Ham Sandwich Loaf

Fill a hollowed-out loaf with shredded chicken, ham, mayonnaise and cheese – chill well then cut into fascinating slices!

Serves 8

INGREDIENTS

6" bread loaf
250 g/8 oz chicken
100 g/3 oz ham - chopped finely
½ cup frozen peas, ½ cup frozen corn
½ cup finely chopped carrots
¼ cup mayonnaise
¼ cup grated cheddar cheese
salt to taste, ½ tsp pepper
½ tsp red chilli flakes
1 tsp mustard powder

METHOD

1. Boil 2 cups water with 1 tsp salt. Add carrots. Boil for 1-2 minutes till crisp tender. Remove from heat. Add peas and corn to the hot water. Strain after 2-3 minutes.

2. Place chicken in a microproof dish. Add ¼ cup water and ¼ tsp salt. Cover with a plastic wrap and microwave for 4 minutes. Remove from microwave and let it cool. Shred chicken into small pieces.

3. Mix the cooked chicken pieces, ham, vegetables, mayonnaise and cheese to get a thick mixture. Add salt, pepper and mustard to taste.

4. Mark a window on the ends of the loaf with a long bread knife. Insert the knife on all four sides, going deep carefully. Insert the knife from both ends. Remove the centre portion to get a hollow, leaving 1 inch shell all around.

5. Fill the meat mixture into the loaf. Close the windows on both sides with a thin slice cut from the scooped portion. Wrap the whole loaf tightly in a cling wrap and chill for 1 hour for the filling to set. To serve, cut into slices.

Sandwich Faces

Children will squeal in delight when they are offered these funny faces to eat!
Makes 12

INGREDIENTS

6 slices of brown bread and 6 slices of white bread - all cut into circles with a cookie cutter or a sharp lid
butter - enough to spread
1 cup finely shredded cabbage

FILLINGS
2 tbsp any jam
2 tbsp mint chutney
2 tbsp cheese spread/cream cheese

FACE
1 carrot - finely grated (for hair)
¼ bell pepper - cut into tiny squares (for eyes)
6 glace cherries - cut into half (for nose)
a firm tomato - cut into small thickish strips (for mouth)

METHOD

1. Cut two circles from each slice of white and brown bread. Butter all circles. Spread jam on two brown circles and cover each brown circle with a white circle. Similarly make round sandwiches of white and brown bread with chutney and also with cheese. Keep aside.

2. Sprinkle shredded cabbage on a platter. Place the sandwiches with the white side up, on the bed of cabbage or lettuce, leaving at least an inch between one another.

3. To make faces, arrange a few shreds of finely grated carrot on the top ¼ portion of the sandwich rounds to make the hair.

4. Place ½ of a glace cherry to make the nose.

5. Arrange tiny squares of green peppers for the eyes. Cut a small, semi circled, thickish strip from a tomato for the mouth. Serve.

Cheese Pockets

Cut a pizza base into triangles; use two kinds of cheese to fill and to cover the triangles; flavour with oregano and chilli flakes – watch these pockets disappear off the plate!

Serves 4

INGREDIENTS

1 thick pizza base, preferably whole wheat
½ cup grated mozzarella cheese
¼ cup grated cheddar cheese
1 tsp oregano, 1 tbsp butter
red chilli flakes or a few freshly crushed peppercorns, optional

METHOD

1. Heat oven to 200°C/400°F.

2. Cut the pizza base into half and then each half into half again to get 4 triangles. Split each triangle from the pointed end almost till the edge, leaving the edges intact, to get a pocket.

3. Mix both the cheeses and oregano.

4. Fill the pockets with cheese mixture, keeping aside some for the top.

5. Place on a rack covered with aluminium foil or a baking tray. Brush the triangles generously with butter.

6. Sprinkle left over cheese. Sprinkle some red chilli flakes or pepper. Keep in the preheated oven for 5-6 minutes until slightly brown and crisp. Cut each piece into 3 thin pieces with a pizza cutter. Serve hot.

Bean Teen Burgers

Buttered crisp buns make tasty containers for a mixture of baked beans, veggies and melting cheese – every child's favourite!

Serves 4

INGREDIENTS

2 tbsp oil
2 onions - chopped finely (1 cup)
1 green bell pepper - chopped fine (½ cup)
200 g/7 oz can baked beans (1¼ cups)
½ tsp pepper and salt
½ tsp chilli sauce
4 soft burger buns
2 tbsp butter
2 cubes cheddar cheese - grated (½ cup)

METHOD

1. Divide buns into two halves. Scoop out, leaving ½" border all around.

2. Heat oil in a pan and fry the onions until softened.

3. Add bell peppers. Stir for 1 minute. Remove from heat. Add baked beans.

4. Add salt, pepper and chilli sauce.

5. Toast the scooped sides on a non-stick pan with some butter.

6. Pile some bean mixture in the scooped out hollows. Grate some cheese over it. Grill or microwave on medium power for 30 seconds.

GLOSSARY OF NAMES/TERMS

HINDI OR ENGLISH NAMES AS USED IN INDIA	ENGLISH NAMES AS USED IN USA/UK/ OTHER COUNTRIES
Aloo	Potatoes
Badaam	Almonds
Capsicum	Bell peppers
Choti Elaichi	Green cardamom
Chilli powder	Red chilli powder, Cayenne pepper
Cornflour	Cornstarch
Coriander, fresh	Cilantro
Cream	Whipping cream
Dalchini	Cinnamon
Degi Mirch	Paprika
Elaichi	Cardamom
Gajar	Carrots
Hara Dhania	Cilantro/fresh or green coriander
Hara Pyaz	Spring onions
Hari Mirch	Green hot peppers, green chillies, serrano peppers
Jeera Powder	Ground cumin seeds
Jhinga	Shrimps
Kaju	Cashewnuts
Khumb	Mushrooms
Kishmish	Raisins
Maida	All purpose flour, Plain flour
Makai, Makki	Corn
Matar	Peas
Nimbu	Lemon
Paneer	Home made cheese made by curdling milk with vinegar or lemon juice. Fresh home made ricotta cheese can be substituted.
Pyaz, pyaaz	Onions
Red chilli flakes	Red pepper flakes
Saboot Kali mirch	Peppercorns
Saunf	Fennel
Sirka	Vinegar
Soda bicarb	Baking soda
Spring Onions	Green onions, Scallions
Suji	Semolina
Til	Sesame seeds
Zaitoon	Olives